C000176051

MY FIRST GUIDE TO BITCOIN

An Easy Read On The Cryptic Topic

Andrew O'Neil

hippocryptical publishing

INTRODUCTION

It's been a decade since Bitcoin was invented, but many people still don't know what it is. This radically new concept and financial environment is not like anything man has ever known. Discovering and understanding the many details may seem daunting. Enter this nifty, little book. This is a light read that will explain the concepts and practicals of Bitcoin.

Disclaimer: Do not take this as professional advice to purchase or mine bitcoin. (It is my unprofessional advice.)

With all seriousness, in the short term, Bitcoin has its ups and downs. Be practical and use your logic for business decisions, not your emotions. It would be a pity to invest in the future with money that you currently need for life expenses. This is true regarding all investments.

And as always, if this is a true medical emergency, please hang up and dial 9-1-1.

CONTENTS

THE BEGINNING

"Dang it boy! Get on with it, you gotta start somewhere!"

GRANDPA JOEL

There once was a person called Satoshi Nakamoto. At least that's the pseudonym he went by. We don't know his real name, nor if it was one person or a group of people. The setting is back in 2008, during the Great Recession. The banks and large financial institutions were blamed for leading the society into a major financial crisis. Countries around the globe suffered from the recession for years afterwards. It was bad stuff. (To be honest, I was a young sprout back then and don't really remember this stuff.) But these are the facts, and it sets the stage for our Satoshi. The plot thickens!

Governments around the world intervened and started doing bail outs. They turned on the machines and the money printers went "BRRRRRRR!" Free money for the banks to stay afloat, WAHOO! But not everyone was in favor of the government's artificial intervention.

These hard times got Satoshi Nakamoto thinking. He devised a plan for a currency that wasn't like fiat (fiat is money that's issued by the government). Nakamoto's currency wouldn't have the government at its center. His currency would be decentralized. Instead it would depend on the people, and the people would control and use it at their own discretion. There would be no authority that could choose to print or destroy the money. He described this as a "peer-to-peer electronic cash system" that doesn't require a third party. You can safely transfer money to anyone in the world without needing any other party. (No banks, no money wiring companies and no blasted credit cards.)

(Sidebar: This was not the first time the idea of a cryptocurrency was thought of. In the 80's and 90's, different people thought of and suggested various cryptocurrency ideas. One of them formulated the concept of proof-of-work to confirm transactions. But Nakamoto's brainchild was unique because he mapped out the practical implementation for this to be a functioning, productive currency.)

Thus Bitcoin was born! Nakamoto wrote out the foundations for Bitcoin in a nine page document that is referred to as The Whitepaper. You can think of this document as the Constitution...just more important. (I'm sorry, I'm sorry. It was just a joke.) It was made public through the cryptography mailing list metzdowd.com on the date of October 31, 2008. Spooky, huh? He planned ahead and had already registered the domain bitcoin.org in August. In the following months, he collaborated with people to revise and improve the system. On January 3, 2009, the first block of the bitcoin system was mined. This was the beginning.

Fun Fact: "Satoshi Nakamoto" in Japanese means central intelligence. It is an appropriate pseudonym, because instead of having a central authority controlling the currency, bitcoin's wise protocol is the inner framework and support for it to be maintained and used by the public.

IT'S ALL MINE

"I think they're playing mined games on me"

Nakamoto designed the Bitcoin system to be self-maintaining. The peer-to-peer transactions have to be verified, to make sure people are giving real bitcoins to each other and not cheating each other. Here is where the mining comes in. Mining is critical in bitcoin's "blockchain."

No, don't close the book! I won't go into boring, intricate details. Please bear with me while we briefly discuss the blockchain system.

To put it simply, the bitcoin network has multiple

computers that choose to be part of the bitcoin system. The computers make a block approximately every 10 minutes. The bitcoin transactions that we make are recorded in the blocks. That's all!

Here's an example (this is just for illustration, there are more factors involved): At 10:00 AM I pay you 1 bitcoin. So in the next block, our transaction will be recorded (along with a lot of other transactions). Let's say the 10:00-10:10 block is block # 238. Now forever it will be recorded in block 238 that I paid you 1 bitcoin. And then the next block will be 239 and it will record other transactions. Block 239 is built on top of the last block of 238. And then the next block and the next one. It's called blockchain because every block is built on the previous one. So it makes a long chain. And every transaction in every block remains recorded permanently. (Currently, we're standing at block 631000.)

Making the blocks is called "mining." The computer that mines the block gets a reward (bitcoins). This is where new bitcoins are minted. But bitcoin's hardcode ensures that computers won't mine blocks too fast and claim all of the bitcoins. The computers have to solve a cryptographic puzzle in order to produce a block. So at 10:10, when block 238 is mined, all of the computers hear about it and race to solve block 239. Whoever solves the puzzle for block 239 first announces it on the network and gets the bitcoin reward. Companies around the world spend a lot of money (millions of dollars) building huge systems of computers just to solve these puzzles and mine blocks. They're doing it to win bitcoins, but everyone benefits because this is confirming our transactions and making the currency run smoothly. Win-win situation.

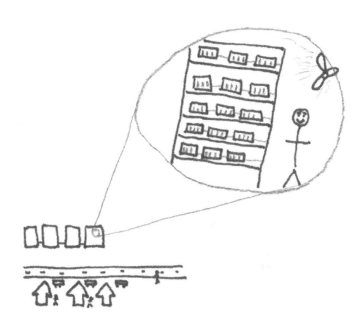

Interesting Point: Bitcoin's protocol is set to make it act differently than fiat. Fiat is generally subject to inflation as time progresses, but bitcoin is expected to experience deflation. The amount of new bitcoin introduced with every block decreases over time. So the influx gradually trickles down, and the value of each bitcoin rises. Also, it is set in the hard-code to stop at 21 million bitcoins. Once that number is reached, people will have to make do with the finite supply of the currency. The constraint of supply while demand continues to rise would increase its value.

Fun Fact: Just like dollars and euros are broken down to cents, and pounds have pence, bitcoin is also made up of smaller pieces: satoshis. (I wonder where that term came from.) But since a single bitcoin may be worth a vast amount of fiat, the smaller sat (satoshi) units aren't just 1/100ths of a bitcoin. Actually, there are 100,000,000 satoshis in a bitcoin! So if you own 0.5 BTC, you own 50,000,000 sats. You're a sats millionaire.

(By the way, BTC is the abbreviation for bitcoin.)

WHAT ABOUT THE COMMONERS?

"If they don't have bread, let them eat cake"

MARIE ANTOINETTE, FRENCH QUEEN

So the companies that have huge mining facilities get bitcoin by mining it. But a common person won't be able to mine a block with his own computer. So where will she get her bitcoins?

There are a few possible routes. One option is: If you can't beat 'em, join 'em! Some of the mining companies allow anyone to join forces with them. It's called a mining pool. Even though they have their huge specialized ASIC mining systems, you can connect with them and take part in trying to figure out the puzzle and mine a block. But it's practically useless to take this route. Because even if you buy the best computer in your electronics store, it won't hold a candle to the torrential power of the mining machines. Their computer system is built differently than our computers, and are vastly more powerful at mining. It's guaranteed that you will lose money on electricity over any meager share of bitcoin you'd get.

So if mining isn't feasible, what is? You can buy bitcoin with your fiat. One option is to buy from a cryptocurrency exchange. It's similar to your country's securities exchange. There are people with dollars trying to buy bitcoin, and there are people trying to sell their bitcoin. If the going rate is 8,000 dollars per bitcoin, there'll be an order book of buyers posting bid orders for 7990, 7995, etc. And there'll be sellers that are asking for 8005, 8010, etc. You deposit your money (or even use a credit card with some exchanges) and choose how much you want to buy and at what rate. If your order is met, voila, you've got it!

In contrast with exchanges, there are websites and apps that sell bitcoin directly to the customer. Their going rate may include a surcharge and certain fees, but some choose these vendors due to the convenience. Some websites may allow credit card purchases with an additional fee.

Interesting Story: Bitstamp, a bitcoin exchange, was dealing with a lot of bitcoins. They wanted to prove to their clientele that they were honest and keeping in store every bitcoin that is being held by them. (This ain't no Ponzi Scheme.) So on May 24, 2014, they made a bitcoin transaction transferring all of the bitcoins they held to another address. This was a public display of the transfer of 183,497 BTC. You can view the transaction by searching the transaction id 057089cd-b9b61b51c3ded3662c3a0665641c1e72ef-219fe59b3f4010c450e779

However, there is a prerequisite for dealing with exchanges. Exchanges usually require KYC. No, that's not fried chicken. KYC stands for Know Your Customer. The government wants to keep track of the money that's going through the exchange and where it's going to. So the exchange is required to ID their customers. So before the exchange allows you to purchase bitcoin, they require proper identification. They may ask for a photo of your passport or of your driver license. Not always, but some require a webcam photo of you also.

I haven't seen this next venue discussed on the forums , but I've seen at money wiring shops (these places sometimes cash checks also) a sign that says

"Buy Bitcoin Here." So that may be a brick and mortar store where you can purchase bitcoin.

Another option is to use a peer-to-peer exchange. The website gives you a listing of other private users that want to trade bitcoin and fiat (remember, fiat is the local currency issued by the government). The website is meant to facilitate this exchange of funds. I've heard that things can be a little sketch, so make sure you do your research if you're taking this route. You don't want to be out of your money with no bitcoins in your hands.

It's technically possible to trade with people you personally know, without even using a third-party network. But you really gotta trust them, otherwise, greed may take over and you just lost a friend, and more importantly, 500 dollars.

Another option that may surprise you is that there are bitcoin ATMs. You can hop on over to this ATM machine and put in some money and it'll send bitcoin to you. They may also require KYC. Be warned that they usually have a higher exchange rate (the ATM is charging you more than what the exchange would've charged you) and may limit how much bitcoin you can purchase.

Fun Fact: There are bitcoin ATMs around the world, from Zimbabwe to Australia!

And the last option we'll discuss is that YOU can choose to be paid in bitcoin. I mean, it is a currency after all. Duhh! So if you have something you'd like to sell, or work that you can provide, you can request to be paid in bitcoin. The client will pay you with bitcoin and you'll be on your merry way.

DELETE COOKIES?!

"Join the Bitcoin side, we have cookies"

OVER-ZEALOUS BITCOIN GEEK

Don't Put Your Money Where Your Mouth Is

Some of you may be wondering: Can I delete my bitcoins by accident? Or what if my computer crashes. I've lost data before, who says I won't lose my 500 dollars worth of bitcoin? And what if someone steals my computer, do they have all of my bitcoins?

Those are good questions. First of all, let's clarify

that bitcoin is NOT saved in your computer. Remember the blockchain we discussed? All of the bitcoins that have been sent to your account are permanently recorded in the worldwide blockchain. (Don't worry, there is some privacy involved in the transactions, so others won't know how much bitcoin you own.)

(I'll try to proceed as simply as possible, while still getting the point across.)

The blockchain records that you received bitcoin. What stops others from taking the bitcoin that you own? Every user has a "bitcoin wallet." It can be stored on your computer, on your phone, or on a dedicated USB hardware wallet. The wallet is just a way for you to save and use your private keys.

The only person that can spend your bitcoins is the person that has your private keys. Just like your car. The only person that can drive and take your car is the person who has the key for it. So as long as you keep your private keys secure, your bitcoin is inaccessible to every living being.

(But young disciple, you may persist in asking: What if a hacker breaks into my computer and extracts my private keys? That needs quite a bit of discussion regarding proper digital hygiene. But I can't leave you hanging, so I'll give you a short answer: To protect against that possibility, get a bitcoin hardware wallet.)

Help, I Can't Feel My Bitcoins!

Ok, everything until now was nice in theory. But here is where people freak out about putting the pedal to the metal. This may be one of the greatest impediments for acceptance of bitcoin:

When I fork over a lot of money for bitcoins, I understand that they're officially in my account. But it's not like cash. I can't hold it, smell it, or rub it all over my face before I go to bed. It doesn't feel right that my money is locked into some distant cyberworld.

Yes, yes, I understand that bitcoin is different than the currency you've been using until now. At first glance, bitcoin seems more like the gold you get in video games than the dollars you get in real life.

Before anything, it's important to acknowledge that bitcoin *is* radically different than fiat. Yes, it will take time to get used to the concept that we have access to a non-government issued currency. And this currency is not physically printed at a centralized location.

However, the emotional issue of not being able to hold bitcoins in your hands shouldn't be a deterrent. Once a person has come to terms with a given currency, he doesn't care if he's tangibly holding it in his hands or not. Many people are paid by their employers through direct deposit into their bank accounts. They never see the dollar bills they received, nor do they ever hold them. But the confirmation of the computer telling them that there are more dollars in their account gives full assurance that they have received the compensation.

So once a person has been oriented with the concept that bitcoin is another currency with value, then seeing the increase of bitcoin in their account should psychologically feel equivalent to receiving a direct deposit.

(TLDR: bitcoin = money in the bank)

DO PEOPLE REALLY DO THIS STUFF

"If all of your friends would jump off a cliff, would you do it too?"

"Chaaa! It's called hang gliding!"

Can I just go and use bitcoin to buy things from stores?
If you're over 18, then yes.

With all seriousness, there aren't many vendors that accept bitcoin as payment...yet. Bear in mind that Bitcoin is still in its early years. Things may drastically change in the coming years, as cryptocurrency develops further. Even the digital payment of fiat, such as Google Pay and Apple Pay, are taking a long time to be adopted by the population. Anyhow, we'll discuss some of the current options for paying with bitcoin.

If you want to pay the store directly with bitcoin, you can search online for stores that accept bitcoin payment. One website that has an extensive database is coinmap.org. Another idea is to google "(restaurant/electronics store/etc.) that accepts cryptocurrency." There are also some online stores that accept bitcoin.

If you're not so bent on the vendor personally accepting your bitcoin, you will have more options. You can buy gift cards for your favorite stores/websites with your bitcoin. Some of the websites will sell the gift cards at a nice discount. There are also browser extensions that make it seamless and easy to make the purchase while shopping on your favorite website.

I've read about some crypto companies providing VISA debit cards to their users. This would make your bitcoin accepted everywhere, because the vendor is just swiping a VISA debit card for the purchase. On your end, you have to refill your account with bitcoin or fiat, and then you can continue using your debit card wherever pleases you.

Remember, just like you wouldn't hand over your fiat money to a random website/app before confirming they are genuine and trustworthy, treat your bitcoin money the same way. Make sure you research if this is a safe company to trust your funds with. Losing money is not fund.

ALTERNATE COINS

"Speak softly and carry a big stick"

THEODORE ROOSEVELT, AMERICAN PRESIDENT

This topic is a little taboo, so I will try to proceed cautiously. I am just presenting the information. You, wise reader, must independently formulate an opinion on the matter...or not. You can choose to just ignore them.

Onwards, Sire! Alright, we understand that the invention and adoption of bitcoin was a revolutionary event. This is the first form of decentralized currency that received widespread acceptance, and it has reached a market capitalization of over 150 billion dollars. This is a form of payment that provides privacy to its users. People saw the potential of this cryptocurrency and how it was gaining traction, so they made other cryptocurrencies. When discussing Bitcoin's copycats, one can appropriately say, "Often imitated, never intimidated."

While some of the cryptocurrencies are simply break offs from bitcoin, others are separate projects started on a clean slate. Break offs from bitcoin are known as hard forks. Developers argued to introduce a change in the system, and forked off to make their own system. They labeled their fork with a name that contained bitcoin and a suffix. But the forks haven't reached anywhere near the same recognition and value as good old Bitcoin.

Besides for bitcoin forks, there are a lot of other cryptocurrencies and tokens. Some trade for less than others. In contrast to the famous currency called "bitcoin", some people call them... "s...doody-coin" (this book adheres to language appropriate for all audiences). As of June 2020, there are 5534 cryptocurrencies. Some are trading for 1/10,000th of a cent. And they're not even worth that much. (Oops, I said something slightly controversial!) Just like people buy penny stocks with dreams of them going big one day, people will pay that cent for 10,000 coins hoping they'll go up one day. If you're contemplating buying some lesser known cryptos, be wary of misleading price rises, because they may be a result of "pump and dump" manipulations.

CRYPTO BIZ MO

"We've got what it takes to take what you've got!"

AUSTRALIAN TAXATION OFFICE

Like all fun and exciting things, there's a non-silver lining somewhere. This chapter briefly discusses a couple of bitcoin's legal aspects.
(Disclaimer: Do not take this as legal advice. Always do proper research to ensure you're following the law.)

Do I have to pay taxes when my bitcoin goes up in value?
We won't discuss the specific laws of every country. But in general, you will probably have to pay taxes when the bitcoin leaves your hands. It is a tax-

able event whether you're exchanging the bitcoin for fiat, other cryptocurrencies, goods, or services. Your country's tax code will determine if your particular transaction will incur a tax, and if yes, how much it would be.

But some countries reduce the tax if you hold onto your bitcoin for more than a year. Many bitcoin holders fall into this category. They're investing their fiat into bitcoin because they believe bitcoin will continue to rise in value. (Similar to the way that people invest their fiat into stocks or commodities, instead of leaving the fiat in the bank. Many private investors have a diversified portfolio that includes bitcoin.) The crypto world coined the term hodl. It means to buy and hold the crypto.

Theories of its origin have suggested it simply being a misspelling that caught on with the hooligans, or that it's a backronym for: Hold On [for] Deal Life.

Note: The issue of tax liability on cryptocurrencies has gotten some folks into a serious mess. Beginners have experimented with cryptotrading (trading cryptocurrencies for each other on an exchange) for a while, only to realize at tax season that every single one of those trades were taxable events. Some of them even lost their money in bad trades and still owed taxes! You can google for a couple scary stories of people owing a lot more taxes than all of the assets and cash they owned. As the saying goes, "know before you go."

Another important topic is privacy. Bitcoin does give some privacy to the sender and receiver. When I pay you some bitcoin, all I need to know about you is your bitcoin public address which is just a string of letters and numbers. And all you know about me is my bitcoin public address. Very, very anonymous. But, don't get any funny ideas! The government is smart and hires firms that help them track the path of bitcoin. This does help them for taxation purposes, but it also helps the government monitor for illegal purchases and money laundering. Stay safe, and enjoy bitcoin responsibly.

While we're on the topic of criminal activity, I'll remind you to beware of fraudsters. We've all heard of the frauds with fiat. For example, a scammer will tell you that she's an African princess that needs x amount of money immediately, and will repay you handsomely in a few days. (Never give money to anyone that you don't know or have reason to trust.) Similarly, there are people trying to steal bit-coin. They may promise to double your bitcoin in 24 hours,if you just hand it over for the 24 hour period. Or that they need to borrow it for a very pressing need and will repay you much more in the future. Treat your bitcoin like your fiat and you will be safe.

THE HALVING

"We half to keep bitcoin going"

Hardwired into the bitcoin system is the monumental halving. At specific milestones, a halving occurs and the blockchain continues. You may have heard about the recent halving that occured on May 11, 2020. So here's what the hype was all about.

We discussed how the miners are creating a new block approximately every ten minutes. They do this hard work in order to receive a reward of bitcoin. Their reward consists of two things: a prize for creating the block, and the sum of all transaction fees contained in their block. Bitcoin's protocol has similarities to gold. Gold needs to be mined out by a laboring entity. And that entity acquires the gold they mined. When man first engaged in mining, Earth had greater and more accessible reserves of gold, so his effort procured a large payload. But as time progresses, the same amount of effort (of seeking out and mining) obtains less of the precious substance. So, too, with bitcoin.

After 210,000 blocks have been mined, the block reward halves. That is estimated to happen every four years. Originally, the block reward started at 50 bitcoins. Miners received 50 BTC for every block they mined. The first halving took place on November 8, 2012, reducing the reward to 25 BTC. Then the second halving occured on July 9, 2016, splitting the reward to only 12.5 BTC. The last halving was on May 11, 2020. You guessed it, 6.25 BTC.

Warning, economics discussion ensues
You may be wondering why it's fair that as the miners keep on working, their salary keeps getting reduced. If anything they should get a raise! Let's go back to our gold analogy. When gold becomes more scarce and it becomes harder to find and mine, does everyone give up on mining it? No! Gold had a certain value when it was being circulated into the world at a faster pace, and when that pace slows, the value of gold increases. Assuming that the usage/desire of gold stays relatively stable, the drop in supply will increase the value. People have to outbid to get the existing supply. The old "supply and

demand" mantra. So even if the miners only extract half of the yellow metal, they very well could be acquiring the same amount of wealth (or more) that they were gaining in the good old days.

Also with bitcoin, the miners are the ones that create bitcoins and release them into the economy. At the beginning, they were releasing a large flow of bitcoin into the world. However, the eventual halvings restrict the influx of bitcoins, and the economy has to make do with the limited supply. When the demand continues its steady increase, even though the new supply is diminishing, bitcoin's value increases. So the miners may only be receiving a prize of 6.25 BTC, but that's worth 60,000 dollars.

Fun Fact: On May 22, 2010, Laszlo Hanyecz made the first ever bitcoin purchase of physical goods. He bought 2 pizzas in Florida for 10,000 BTC!

APPENDIX

For sanity's sake, I'll keep this really short.
If you'd like to see "The White Paper" of bitcoin,
you can visit hippocryptical.com to see it.

I hope to soon add other resources and helpful tips
on the website.

NOTE FROM THE AUTHOR

I hope you enjoyed reading *My First Guide To Bitcoin*. I'm a small independent author, and I put a lot of time and effort into making this book.

Did this book teach you new things? Did you enjoy a good chuckle? I'd love to hear about it, and your review helps other readers find new books that suit their needs. Please share your experience by writing a review on Amazon.

Thank you

Printed in Great Britain
by Amazon